BEST
DUMP &
FREEZE
TREATS

BEST
DUMP &
FREEZE
TREATS

FROZEN FRUIT SALADS, PIES, FLUFFS, AND MORE RETRO DESSERTS

MONICA SWEENEY

THE COUNTRYMAN PRESS

A DIVISION OF W. W. NORTON & COMPANY

INDEPENDENT PUBLISHERS SINCE 1923

Photo Credits:
All photos by Allan Penn, unless otherwise noted below.
Pages 10, 11: © Irina Bg/Shutterstock.com; 23: © Sea Wave/Shutterstock.com;
37: © jrelka/iStockphoto.com; 40, 41: © amerleeknight/iStockphoto.com; 46: © Irina_
Meliukh/iStockphoto.com; 54, 55: © Natalia Van Doninck/iStockphoto.com;
67: © picalotta/iStockphoto.com; 83: © Lecic/iStockphoto.com; 86, 87: © bhofack/
iStockphoto.com; 93: © Oksana Struk/iStockphoto.com; 98: © pearl7/Shutterstock
.com; 106, 107: © Andrea Carpedi/iStockphoto.com

Front Cover: © LeeAnnWhite/iStockphoto.com; © Lauren King/iStockphoto.com;
© Davydenko Yuliia/Shutterstock.com
Spine: © Kitch Bain/Shutterstock.com
Back Cover: © Natalia Van Doninck/iStockphoto.com; Allan Penn

For information about permission to reproduce selections from this book, write to
Permissions, The Countryman Press, 500 Fifth Avenue, New York, NY 10110

For information about special discounts for bulk purchases, please contact
W. W. Norton Special Sales at specialsales@wwnorton.com or 800-233-4830.

The Countryman Press
www.countrymanpress.com

A division of W. W. Norton & Company, Inc.,
500 Fifth Avenue, New York, NY 10110
www.wwnorton.com

ISBN 978-1-58157-364-0 (pbk.)

10 9 8 7 6 5 4 3 2 1

TO ALLAN,
FOR PUTTING THE "ZEN"
IN FROZEN TREATS

BEST DUMP & FREEZE TREATS
CONTENTS

Chapter Four: Frozen Pies / 87

Chapter Five: Frozen Cakes/ 107

Introduction

This dump-and-freeze collection of America's best retro desserts takes you back to a time when guilty pleasures were nothing to feel guilty about and effortless desserts were a source of pride. Frozen treats were at the peak of their popularity during the 1950s and '60s. Americans were accustomed to their stockpiled canned goods and were thrilled to discover new prepackaged food items, simple recipes, and kitchen appliances that saved them precious time. With this renewed focus on convenience, it's no surprise that frozen treats prepared with just a few key ingredients and in just a few minutes were making their mark. While times have changed since the freezer-friendly treats in this book were popular, the old-fashioned principles of cooking and entertaining remain surprisingly relevant: Simple is better, convenience is a must, and presentation is key.

Let's start with the simple part: Many of the dump-and-freeze recipes in this book include no more than five or six ingredients, which means you can throw them together with less mess and fewer trips to the grocery store. As if that weren't enough, none of them require even a minute of baking, so they're perfectly suited to a hot summer day. If convenience and affordability are as important to you as they were to the mid-century homemaker, you'll be happy to discover that the ingredients for these recipes often come in a bag, a box, or a can: Think frozen whipped topping, canned pie filling, pudding mix, and sweetened condensed milk. Last but not least, presentation is the cornerstone of retro desserts. While the ingredients may be basic, the presentation of your frozen dessert should show that you care. Alongside some of my favorite recipes, I'll share some simple tips for adding a dash of style and sophistication to your finished product.

Now you're ready to travel back in time and re-create the niftiest dump-and-freeze treats that America's rock-and-roll decades had to offer. Jumpstart your culinary joy ride with a wonderfully peculiar favorite: the frozen fruit salad. This sweet treat, sometimes referred to as a fluff, begins with a delectable cream base (like Cool Whip) and includes all your favorite fruits whirled inside. Next, venture into the world of frozen bars and combine classic flavors like mint-chocolate, peanut butter, and butterscotch with the crunch of all-American cereals and buttery cookie crusts. Dump-and-freeze your way to a groovy assortment of frozen pops, chilled drinks, and ice cream pie recipes and bring back fond memories of the great American 1950s soda fountain. Finish out this neat collection with some old-fashioned freezer cakes. It's time to go retro. Clear out your freezer and leave plenty of room for the coolest desserts the past has to offer!

CHAPTER ONE

SALADS & FLUFFS

Classic Frozen Salad

When was the last time you got to eat dessert with your meal instead of after it? If your answer is the 1950s, then you're not alone. Back then, a sweet fruit salad like this one was a perfectly acceptable side dish. Experience the culinary boldness of that daring decade yourself with this surprising addition to an otherwise ordinary meal.

Yield: 10 servings

1 (8-ounce) package cream cheese, softened

1 cup mayonnaise

1 (20-ounce) can fruit cocktail, drained

½ cup maraschino cherries

1 cup heavy cream, whipped

1½ cups mini marshmallows

Mix together cream cheese and mayonnaise until well blended. Add the fruit cocktail, cherries, whipped cream, and marshmallows. Spoon salad mixture into a Bundt cake pan lined with plastic wrap. Freeze for 4 hours or more (preferably overnight). Unmold onto a platter before serving. Cover in more whipped cream if desired and garnish with extra cherries and marshmallows.

Cherry Supreme Salad

Whether you debut this dessert at a baby shower or a family gathering, people will swoon over its unique appearance and frozen goodness. Mix in your favorite nuts for a crunchy surprise that's old-fashioned in every way or skip the nuts and enjoy it smooth and simple.

Yield: 18 servings

1 (20-ounce) can cherry pie filling

1 (20-ounce) can crushed pineapple, drained

1 (11-ounce) can mandarin oranges, drained

1 (14-ounce) can sweetened condensed milk

1 (12-ounce) container Cool Whip

¼ cup lemon juice

⅔ cup chopped walnuts

In a large bowl, combine all ingredients, stirring in walnuts last. Pour into a 9 x 13-inch baking dish or individual serving bowls. Place in freezer for 4 or more hours. Remove from freezer 10 to 15 minutes before serving. Garnish with extra nuts or cherries.

Pistachio Fluff
Salad

Pistachio is a genuinely retro flavor that's rarely used in modern desserts. Bring it back to life with this pleasing green fluff that stayed popular until the 1970s (when it was renamed "Watergate Salad" for its stash of hidden surprises). The surprises tucked away in this Pistachio Fluff include tiny marshmallows and tender coconut flakes.

Yield: 10 servings

1 (3.4-ounce) package pistachio instant pudding mix

1 (8-ounce) container Cool Whip

1 (20-ounce) can crushed pineapple, drained

1 cup mini marshmallows

¼ cup flaked sweetened coconut

In a large bowl, combine pudding mix, Cool Whip, and crushed pineapple. Stir in marshmallows and coconut flakes. Cover and freeze until firm.

WOW FACTOR
Try serving this dessert in fabulously retro tulip-shape sundae glasses with long-handled spoons. You can also alternate layers of Pistachio Fluff and Cool Whip. A sprinkle of pistachios on top gives you extra points for presentation.

Berry Cyclone Frozen Salad

Marshmallow spread may be a great supporting actor here, but the berries have the lead role. Invite some friends over for a black-and-white movie and complete the retro theme with this nostalgic dessert. Swap in your favorite berries, fresh or frozen, to make it your own.

Yield: 16 servings

1 cup heavy cream

1 cup Marshmallow Fluff

1 (8-ounce) package cream cheese, softened

¼ cup mayonnaise

1 cup canned fruit cocktail, drained

½ cup sliced strawberries

½ cup sliced bananas

½ cup diced pineapple

Mix together ¼ cup heavy cream and Fluff. Stir in cream cheese and mayonnaise. Whip remaining cream until stiff and fold into Fluff mixture. Stir in fruit. Drop into a mold or 9 x 9-inch baking pan and freeze for 4 hours before serving.

WOW FACTOR
Serving individual portions of this fruity salad over a bed of greens with a few slices of strawberry on top will give it true vintage pizzazz.

Maraschino Cocktail Salad

Every day feels like a holiday when you serve this arctic blend of fluffy frozen cream and vibrant red cherries. When you're eager to bring a frosty finish to an otherwise sweltering day, this dump-and-freeze delight is just the thing.

Yield: 8 to 10 servings

2 (8-ounce) packages cream cheese, softened

1 cup mayonnaise

1 cup heavy cream, whipped

½ cup red maraschino cherries, quartered

½ cup green maraschino cherries, quartered (or use all red)

1 (16-ounce) can fruit cocktail, drained

2 cups mini marshmallows

In a large bowl, mix together cream cheese and mayonnaise. Stir in whipped cream, cherries, and fruit cocktail, and fold in marshmallows. Pour into 8 to 10 small trifle dishes or decorative glasses. Freeze until firm. Garnish with whipped cream and leftover maraschino cherries.

Tropical Delight
Salad

Canned pineapples are the cornerstone of many frozen salads of the 1950s, thanks to the energizing burst of flavor and added texture they provide. This frozen delight is a cinch to make and features delicious sliced bananas and crunchy pecans. Take your tongue on a tropical vacation with this retro treat.

Yield: 10 to 12 servings

2 bananas, sliced thin

1 (20-ounce) can crushed pineapple, juice reserved

2 cups sour cream

2 tablespoons lemon juice

¾ cup sugar

⅛ teaspoon salt

¼ cup maraschino cherries, drained and sliced

¼ cup chopped pecans

Allow banana slices to marinate in pineapple juice while preparing this fluff. In a large mixing bowl, combine sour cream, lemon juice, sugar, and salt. Stir in the pineapples, cherries, pecans, and marinated (drained) bananas. Pour into a 9 x 9-inch baking pan and freeze for 4 hours or more.

This festive fluff can also be poured into paper-lined muffin tins or mini trifle dishes for individual appeal. If you have a fresh lemon on hand, add a small curl of lemon peel or a little bit of zest to each serving.

Blueberry-Peach
Frozen Salad

This flavor combination has modern appeal, but the recipe is ripe with nostalgia. Whip up this thick and hearty cream cheese salad for a satisfying end to your all-American meal. Be sure to make an artful design of peaches and berries around this salad to impress your guests before serving. They'll think you slaved over this dessert all day.

Yield: 8 servings

1 (8-ounce) package cream cheese, softened

1 (16-ounce) container sour cream

1 tablespoon lemon juice

½ cup sugar

1 cup canned diced peaches, drained

1 cup fresh blueberries

In a large mixing bowl, blend cream cheese and sour cream. Add lemon juice and sugar and mix until fully combined. Stir in peaches and blueberries. Line a loaf pan or mold with plastic wrap and then spoon mixture into pan. Freeze 4 to 6 hours or until firm. Allow to sit 15 to 20 minutes before inverting dessert onto a serving platter.

WOW FACTOR
Create a decorative border around the base of this unique salad by alternating peach slices and blueberries. You can even top the finished mold with a mound of whipped cream and a sprig of mint.

Wispy White Fluff Salad

This creamy, banana-rich salad features delicate wisps of lush cream, juicy pineapples, tender mashed bananas, and crunchy nuts. These little flavor clouds make a memorable debut when served in decorative cupcake wrappers or long-stemmed glassware. Add a sprinkle of nuts and a few slices of bananas to the top of each delicious serving, and presto—dessert is ready!

Yield: 8 to 10 servings

4 ripe bananas, mashed

1 (8-ounce) can crushed pineapple (including juice)

1 tablespoon lemon juice

¾ cup sugar

¼ teaspoon salt

2 cups sour cream

½ cup chopped walnuts or pecans, divided

Whipped cream, for garnish

Fresh fruit of choice, for garnish

In a large bowl, mix together mashed bananas, pineapple (including the juice), and lemon juice. Add in sugar, salt, and sour cream. Stir until well blended. Stir in ¼ cup nuts. Pour mixture into lined cupcake tins or single-serving dishes. Freeze for 4 to 6 hours, or until firm. Garnish with whipped cream, fresh fruit, and remaining nuts.

Raspberry Dream Fluff Salad

Stay cool with this five-ingredient recipe that can turn a regular meal into a retro-inspired event. When you take three compatible fruit flavors like raspberry, oranges, and lime and you present them in a deliciously creamy whirl of Cool Whip and sweetened milk, you get a lot of well-deserved compliments. Try substituting straw-berries for raspberries if that happens to be your family's fruit of choice.

Yield: 12 to 15 servings

1 (8-ounce) container Cool Whip

1 (14-ounce) can sweetened condensed milk

2 tablespoons lime juice (fresh or bottled)

1 (12-ounce) bag frozen raspberries or 1½ cups fresh raspberries

2 (15-ounce) cans mandarin oranges, drained

In a large bowl, combine the Cool Whip and condensed milk. Add lime juice. Stir in frozen raspberries and oranges. Pour into a 9 x 9-inch baking pan or individual serving dishes and freeze until solid, 4 to 6 hours.

Cherry Salad Cupcakes

This finished dessert is the cherry on top of any meal. With a hint of almond to complement the sweet and tangy combination of cherries and pineapples, you'll fall instantly in love with this chilly blast from the past. Preparation time is just a few minutes, but your mouth will water as you wait for these adorable frozen cupcakes to firm up in the freezer.

Yield: 12 to 18 servings

1 (20-ounce) can crushed pineapple, drained (reserve juice)

2–3 bananas, sliced

1 (12-ounce) container Cool Whip

1 (14-ounce) can sweetened condensed milk

¼ cup lemon juice

¼ teaspoon almond extract

12 maraschino cherries (halved), plus juice

Whipped cream, for garnish

¼ cup sliced almonds, for garnish

In a small bowl, pour pineapple juice over bananas to soak them. Set aside. In a large bowl, mix together Cool Whip, condensed milk, lemon juice, and almond extract. Stir in cherries, 2 tablespoons cherry juice, drained pineapples, and marinated banana slices. Mix well. Scoop mixture into lined cupcake tins. Freeze 4 to 6 hours or until firm. Garnish with whipped cream and almonds before serving.

Pineapple-Strawberry Frozen Salad

If the pale pink hue of this nifty little treat doesn't make it memorable, then the taste will. Packed with the bold flavors of pineapple and strawberry daiquiri, this party confection will fly off the serving platter faster than you can say "dump-and-freeze."

Yield: 10 to 12 servings

1 (8-ounce) package cream cheese, softened

1 (8-ounce) container Cool Whip

1 cup strawberry daiquiri mix

1 (8-ounce) can crushed pineapple, drained

1 (3-ounce) bag chopped walnuts

In a large bowl, using an electric mixer, blend the softened cream cheese with Cool Whip. Add strawberry daiquiri mix and blend until fully combined. Stir in pineapple and chopped walnuts. Pour into a loaf pan or individual serving dishes. Freeze for 4 hours or until firm. Remove from freezer 15 to 20 minutes before serving.

WOW FACTOR
Crank up the presentation of this pink treat when you add a garnish of fresh berries and a basil leaf to each individual portion.

Cranberry-Banana Fluff Salad

Three cheers to the generation that was brave enough to combine ingredients like tangy pineapple, tart cranberry sauce, and sweet cream. This midcentury experiment works and here's why: It features a balanced mix of bold and mild flavors. For that reason and more, it's bound to become a longstanding family recipe.

Yield: 12 to 16 servings

1 (20-ounce) can crushed pineapple, drained

1 (12-ounce) container Cool Whip, plus a dollop for topping

1 cup sour cream

1 (14-ounce) can whole-berry cranberry sauce

¼ cup sugar

4 sliced or mashed bananas

½ cup chopped pecans, divided (optional)

In a large bowl, mix together pineapple, Cool Whip, sour cream, cranberry sauce, and sugar. Stir in bananas and ¼ cup pecans. Spoon into paper-lined muffin tins or serving dishes. Freeze for 4 hours or until firm. Remove from freezer 10 to 15 minutes before serving and top with a dollop of Cool Whip and a sprinkle of pecans, if desired.

Orange-Apricot
Frozen Salad

What's orange and fruity and retro all over? This frozen fluff salad. The addition of apricots adds a lovely twist to a full bouquet of fruit flavors. Serve this over lettuce leaves for a delicate, after-dinner reminder of simpler times.

Yield: 8 to 10 servings

1 (12-ounce) can apricot pie filling

1 (14-ounce) can sweetened condensed milk

1 (8-ounce) container Cool Whip

1 (8-ounce) can crushed pineapple, drained

1 (8-ounce) can mandarin oranges, drained and chopped

1 cup mini marshmallows

In a large bowl, mix together pie filling, condensed milk, and Cool Whip. Stir in pineapple, mandarin oranges, and mini marshmallows. Empty into a plastic wrap-lined loaf pan. Freeze for 4 hours or until firm. Invert onto a serving plate.

Lemon Delight
Frozen Fluff

Pucker up and enjoy this tasty frozen treat made from lemon pie filling and a few other common ingredients that you may already have on hand. Use your instincts to modify this recipe if you're feeling inspired. Try it with or without oranges. Add in ½ cup of blueberries. Toss in 1 cup of mini marshmallows. Put your individual stamp on this recipe and you'll surprise your guests every time you serve it.

Yield: 14 to 16 servings

1 (8-ounce) container Cool Whip

1 (15-ounce) can lemon pie filling

1 (10-ounce) can mandarin oranges, drained

1 (15-ounce) can fruit cocktail, drained

1 (20-ounce) can pineapple tidbits, drained

In a large bowl, mix together Cool Whip and lemon pie filling. Stir in oranges, fruit cocktail, and pineapple. Scoop into individual serving dishes and freeze until firm.

CHAPTER TWO

FROZEN BARS

Crunchy Choco Bars

Chocolate lovers rejoiced in 1958 when the first chocolate rice cereal appeared on supermarket shelves. Its versatility as an ingredient in crunchy baked goods and other fine treats made America's housewives swoon. These bars are an easy way to replicate their sweet success in the kitchen.

Hint: Go chunky with the peanut butter for an even more satisfying crunch.

Yield: 12 servings

½ cup corn syrup

½ cup peanut butter

4 cups chocolate rice cereal

½ cup mini chocolate chips (optional)

In a large bowl, mix together corn syrup and peanut butter. Fold in chocolate rice cereal and chocolate chips, if using. Empty into a greased 9 x 9-inch pan. Using a piece of wax paper, press mixture into an even layer. Place in freezer until firm. Cut into squares and serve.

Butterscotch Layer Bars

The comforting sweetness of butterscotch is the key ingredient in this retro-flavored freezer bar. With four layers in every mouthful—crumbly cracker, smooth cream, rich butterscotch pudding, and airy light topping—this bar deserves a place at the table no matter the decade!

Yield: 12 servings

CRUST

1½ cups graham cracker crumbs

¼ cup sugar

6 tablespoons butter, melted

FILLING

2 (8-ounce) packages cream cheese

3 cups cold whole milk, divided

¼ cup sugar

2 (3.4-ounce) packages instant butterscotch pudding mix

2 cups Cool Whip

In a small bowl, combine the graham cracker crumbs, sugar, and butter. Use wax paper to press the crumb mixture into a greased 9 x 9-inch baking dish. In a medium-size bowl, beat the cream cheese, ¼ cup milk, and sugar until smooth. Spread over crust. Whisk together remaining milk and pudding mix until pudding thickens. Spread pudding over cream cheese layer. Gently spread Cool Whip over pudding. Freeze for 4 hours or until set.

WOW FACTOR
If you've got any mini chocolate chips or butterscotch baking chips on hand, now is the perfect time to use them. Sprinkle them over the finished dessert for a bonus layer of flavor and an impressive presentation.

Chocolate-Peppermint Bark

A recipe similar to this one could be found printed on bags of semisweet chocolate chips in the 1950s. Why not re-create it with this delicious but extremely simple formula for dump-and-freeze success? Experiment by adding family favorites to your chocolate bark, such as mini marshmallows or white chocolate chips!

Yield: 12 servings

2 cups melted semisweet chocolate chips

¾ cup finely chopped peppermint stick candy

¾ cup chopped nuts

Line a baking sheet with wax paper. Melt chocolate chips in the microwave at 15-second intervals or over a double boiler. Fold in peppermint candy and nuts. Pour bark mix over wax paper (aim for a ¼-inch-thick puddle). Allow to freeze for at least 45 minutes. Chop gently into pieces of "bark" and serve.

Peanut Butter
Pretzel Bars

Salty meets sweet in these adult- and kid-friendly freezer bars. It begins with a crunchy layer of ground pretzel sticks soaked in butter and blended with sugar to form the perfect crust. Layer on a thick and creamy peanut butter coating and freeze. A few hours later, you'll be more than ready to experience the best kind of snacking a freezer can provide.

Yield: 12 to 15 servings

CRUST

2 cups finely crushed pretzel sticks

½ cup (1 stick) butter, melted

4 tablespoons sugar

FILLING

1 (8-ounce) package cream cheese

1½ cups powdered sugar

1 cup chunky peanut butter, warmed

1 cup milk

1 (12-ounce) container Cool Whip, divided

2 tablespoons chocolate syrup

¼ cup chopped peanuts, for garnish

In a small bowl, mix together crust ingredients and add to bottom of a 9 x 13-inch baking pan. Press with wax paper to make an even layer. Allow to set in the refrigerator while making the filling. Cream together the cream cheese and powdered sugar. Add in warm peanut butter and milk and mix until fully combined. Fold in 2 cups Cool Whip. Spread mixture over crust and freeze for at least 4 hours. Remove from freezer 20 minutes before serving, frost with remaining Cool Whip, drizzle with syrup, and sprinkle with chopped peanuts.

Butterscotch Crisp Bars

This recipe takes cereal bars to a whole new level of indulgence. Adding butterscotch pudding to a time-tested favorite gives this dump-and-freeze dessert a comforting, homespun flavor. Enjoy these crunchy rice cereal bars straight from the freezer and ruminate about the good old days as you savor every morsel.

Yield: 12 to 15 servings

1 (7.5-ounce) jar Marshmallow Fluff

¼ cup (½ stick) butter

3 tablespoons (about ⅓ of a 3.4-ounce box) butterscotch-flavor instant pudding mix

5 cups rice cereal

Scrape contents of Fluff jar into a large saucepan. Add butter to pan and heat on low, stirring frequently, until fully combined. Remove from burner. Stir in pudding mix and rice cereal. Empty into a 9 x 13-inch baking dish. Use wax paper to help press mixture into an even layer. Freeze for several hours before cutting into squares.

Cornflake Crunchies

You've had the rice cereal equivalent, but this cornflake spinoff brings added volume and crunch. Cereal lovers will rejoice in this wholesome indulgence made up of sweet and gooey marshmallow-coated cornflakes. Throw some almond slices in the mix for a hint of adult sophistication or leave them out and make like a kid again.

Yield: 12 to 15 servings

¾ cup (1½ sticks) salted butter

1 (12-ounce) bag mini marshmallows

1 teaspoon vanilla extract

6 cups cornflakes

1 (5-ounce) bag sliced almonds (optional)

Melt the butter and marshmallows together in the microwave or on the stovetop. Stir in vanilla extract, cornflakes, and almonds. Empty into a greased 9 x 13-inch baking dish. Allow to cool. Freeze and cut into squares to serve.

WOW FACTOR
Make these bars even more festive and indulgent with the addition of rainbow sprinkles or by using pastel-color marshmallows in place of regular marshmallows.

CHAPTER THREE

ICE CREAM TREATS & POPS

Soda Pop Ice Cream

The 1950s soda fountain was a bustling hangout and a prime spot for budding teenage romance. This homemade soda pop ice cream is a tribute to the days when restaurants featured jukeboxes, chrome-plate countertops, and a delicious array of frozen treats to share and enjoy with friends. Made from your favorite soda and sweetened milk, this simple experiment is as cool and simple as it gets.

Yield: 8 to 10 servings

2 (14-ounce) cans sweetened condensed milk

1 (2-liter) bottle carbonated beverage (like orange soda)

In a large bowl or pitcher, mix together milk and carbonated soda. Transfer to a 9 x 13-inch baking pan. Freeze to firmness, approximately 3 hours. Break into pieces and transfer to a large mixing bowl. Beat until smooth, then return to baking pan and cover. Freeze until firm and scoop servings into a mug or bowl. Top with whipped cream and sprinkles if desired.

Old-Fashioned
Popsicles

Nothing says growing up like a Popsicle straight from the freezer. While frozen juice on a stick has been served as a treat since the early twentieth century, Popsicles earned their name and surged in popularity in the '50s and '60s. Make your own frozen tribute to the past with this simple, nostalgic recipe for pops of any flavor.

Yield: 16 servings

1 (3-ounce) box Jell-O gelatin mix

1 (.13-ounce) packet unsweetened Kool-Aid mix

1 cup sugar

1½ cups hot water

2½ cups cold water

In a large mixing bowl or saucepan, dissolve mix powders and sugar in hot water. Add cold water and let sit for 10 minutes. Pour into your favorite Popsicle mold or paper cups. Freeze for 1 to 2 hours and add Popsicle sticks. Freeze until solid.

WOW FACTOR
Today's Popsicle molds are not what they used to be. You can easily order decorative molds shaped like rockets, animals, stars, and jewels; impress your guests when you serve a classic treat with a brand-new look.

Homemade Frozen Fudge Pops

Fudge pops became a sensation in the mid-1940s and they've been part of American culture ever since. It's easy to understand why they rose to fame: A handheld dessert on a stick is irresistibly convenient, while chocolate fudge is a flavor that can't be beat. This frozen treat will remind you to enjoy the little things, especially when the little things are frozen and chocolate.

Yield: 12 servings

1 (4-ounce) package instant chocolate pudding mix

2 cups milk

¼ cup sugar

1 cup canned evaporated milk

Whisk together pudding mix and milk until pudding forms. Stir in sugar and evaporated milk. Pour into Popsicle molds or paper cups. Freeze for 1 hour. Add sticks and freeze until solid.

Fruit Juice Pops

For a fun treat with old-fashioned appeal, these juice pops are just the thing. Swap out the cranberry juice for grape juice if you like and experiment with decorative pop molds. This simple, four-ingredient freezer treat will awaken the kid in you.

Yield: 18 servings

½ can frozen cranberry juice concentrate, thawed

½ can frozen apple juice concentrate, thawed

2 (23-ounce) jars applesauce

½ cup water

Pour juice concentrates into a large mixing bowl. Stir in applesauce and water. Fill paper or plastic cups with mixture. Freeze for 1 hour. Insert sticks; freeze until firm. Remove and allow pops to sit for 3 to 5 minutes before gently twisting out of cups.

Orange Cream Pudding Pops

This cool favorite is proof that sometimes simpler is better. Why get fancy with modern recipes when this tried-and-true Creamsicle is easily one of the best frozen treats around?

Yield: 8 to 10 servings

1 (3-ounce) package orange Jell-O mix

1 cup hot water

1 cup cold water

1 (3.4-ounce) package instant vanilla pudding mix

1 (8-ounce) container Cool Whip

In a large mixing bowl, add Jell-O mix to hot water and stir until powder dissolves. Mix in cold water and allow mixture to cool for 3 to 5 minutes. Stir in powdered pudding mix. Chill for 10 minutes. Fold in Cool Whip. Spoon mixture into Popsicle molds or paper cups and insert sticks after an hour (or when stick is able to stay upright). Freeze until solid and enjoy.

Cherry Soda
Slushie

It's not easy to find a convenience store with slushies on tap—and when you do, they never have your favorite flavor. If you want to enjoy an old-fashioned slushie at home, all you need are a few key ingredients and a blender.

Yield: 1 serving

2 cups crushed ice

1 cup Dr. Pepper (or your favorite soda)

½ teaspoon maraschino cherry juice (or grenadine syrup)

1–2 tablespoons cherry-flavored drink powder

Place ice, soda, cherry juice, and drink powder (1 tablespoon for sweet, 2 tablespoons for extra-sweet) in a blender. Pulse until smooth and pour into a tall glass.

WOW FACTOR
Vintage glassware and mason jars are both great choices when you want to serve this frozen treat with true retro style. Add a colorful straw and slurp away!

Chocolate-Coconut Dream Pops

Many outstanding desserts begin with marshmallows, and this is one of them. You simply take a giant, fluffy marshmallow, spear it with a pretzel stick, and dip it in a layer of melted chocolate and shredded coconut. The end product is an adorable treat you can eat on the go!

Yield: 12 servings

12 pretzel sticks

12 large marshmallows

3 ounces semisweet baking chocolate, melted

½ cup shredded sweetened coconut

Insert a pretzel stick into the flat side of each marshmallow. Carefully dip the other end of each marshmallow in melted chocolate, then shredded coconut, rotating marshmallow slowly to coat. Place on a baking sheet lined with wax or parchment paper and freeze until chocolate is firm.

Frozen Hot Chocolate

Indulgent soda fountain desserts like this one are what made it great to be alive in the '50s. Just dump and blend these five ingredients and you've got yourself a frozen treat you can drink from your favorite mug.

Yield: 1 serving

1 cup cold milk

1 packet hot cocoa mix

2 tablespoons Marshmallow Fluff

1 tablespoon chocolate syrup

6 ice cubes, crushed

Place all ingredients in a blender. Pulse until smooth. Pour into a mug or bowl.

WOW FACTOR
Garnish with whipped cream and a sprinkling of miniature chocolate chips or rainbow sprinkles and you'll maximize both the flavor and the visual appeal!

Bananas Foster Freezer Pops

Bananas Foster became famous in the 1950s when chefs at a New Orleans restaurant would sautée bananas in rum, banana liqueur, and brown sugar and then set the alcohol on fire for a dramatic show. While this recipe does not call for setting fire to anything, it does replicate the sweet banana flavorings that made this dish legendary.

Yield: 4 to 6 servings

2 large ripe bananas, mashed

½ cup Cool Whip

1 teaspoon vanilla extract

½ teaspoon ground cinnamon

¼ teaspoon ground nutmeg

½ teaspoon rum extract

1 tablespoon caramel sauce

In a medium bowl, mix together mashed bananas and Cool Whip. Stir in vanilla, cinnamon, nutmeg, and rum extract until well blended. Add caramel sauce and stir until caramel is lightly swirled into mixture. Spoon mixture into Popsicle molds or paper cups. Freeze for 4 hours or until solid.

Double Butterscotch Pudding Pops

Vintage flavor becomes freezer friendly with this lavish, buttery ice pop. Remember those butterscotch-flavored candies in your grandma's candy dish? This easy-breezy pop recipe lets you enjoy that same nostalgic flavor straight from the freezer.

Yield: 6 servings

1 (3.4-ounce) box butterscotch instant pudding

1 cup cold half-and-half

1 cup cold milk

⅓ cup butterscotch chips

In a medium mixing bowl, whisk together pudding powder, half-and-half, and milk until pudding thickens. Fold in butterscotch chips. Pour into 6 paper cups. Insert a wooden Popsicle stick or plastic spoon in the center of each cup. Freeze for at least 4 hours or until firm. Peel off paper cup and enjoy.

Coconut Rainbow Sherbet

This layered sherbet dessert is a party in a glass. Serve it in elegant or retro dishes and alternate creamy white coconut layers with colorful sherbet so it's as pleasing to the eye as it is to your taste buds. If rainbow sherbet isn't available at the grocery store, find another fun flavor for this retro freezer treat.

Yield: 6 servings

1 pint whipping cream

¼ cup shredded sweetened coconut

1 teaspoon almond extract

2 tablespoons powdered sugar

½ gallon rainbow sherbet

Rainbow sprinkles (for garnish)

In a medium bowl, whip cream until stiff. Add coconut, almond extract, and powdered sugar to whipped cream and stir until combined. Drop a scoop of sherbet into the bottom of small trifle dish or decorative glass. Drop a spoonful of the cream mixture on top. Add an additional scoop of sherbet and a dash of sprinkles and serve immediately, or freeze until ready to serve.

Fast & Frozen
Peach Melba

This recipe is so retro it's vintage. Its roots are in the mid-nineteenth century, but the availability of canned peaches in the 1950s made it popular all over again. Throw it together for your next book club meeting and watch your friends relish its timeless blend of flavors. To make this recipe even tastier, drizzle on bottled strawberry sauce or make a fresh raspberry topping for extra sweetness.

Yield: 4 servings

4 round shortcake dessert shells

4 scoops vanilla ice cream

2 (15-ounce) cans peach halves, drained

1 cup Cool Whip, divided

Sliced almonds, for garnish

SAUCE (OPTIONAL)

1½ cups fresh raspberries

2 tablespoons powdered sugar

1 teaspoon lemon juice

1 teaspoon water

Place dessert shells on a large plate or platter. Add 1 scoop of ice cream to each dessert shell. Arrange a peach half (face down) on the ice cream scoop. Top with ¼ cup Cool Whip and a sprinkle of almonds. Repeat for all dessert shells. Serve immediately.

To make raspberry topping: In a food processor or blender, purée raspberries, sugar, lemon juice, and water until well blended and smooth. Drizzle about 1 tablespoon of sauce over each serving.

Peanuts & Caramel Pops

Remember snacks that advertised a prize in every box? The prize that comes with these retro pops is the joy you'll feel every time you take one out of the freezer. This recipe takes an old-fashioned ballpark snack and reinvents it as a creamy, crunchy ice cream pop.

Yield: 8 servings

1 cup smooth peanut butter, divided

12 chocolate peanut butter cups, chopped

1 quart vanilla ice cream, softened and divided

1 cup caramel sundae sauce, divided

¾ cup salted red-skinned peanuts, chopped and divided

Warm the peanut butter in the microwave for 15 to 20 seconds to make it easier to work with. Drop about 2 tablespoons of warm peanut butter into the bottom of a large plastic or paper cup. Layer on peanut butter cup pieces, ½ cup ice cream, 2 tablespoons caramel sauce, and 1 to 2 tablespoons chopped peanuts. Top with a little extra ice cream to cover the candy. Repeat with remaining 7 cups. Insert wooden Popsicle stick and freeze for 4 to 6 hours before serving. Peel away the paper cup or wiggle free from plastic cup once slightly warmed, and enjoy.

Pineapple-Orange Sherbet

Dump, mix, and freeze your way to this tropical sherbet blend that gives ice cream a run for its money. All it takes is five simple ingredients to make your own Pineapple-Orange Sherbet. Customize this recipe with your favorite flavors. I like to swap out the orange juice for something more exotic, like orange-pineapple-mango juice. Just be sure to mix the ingredients well during the freezing process so that your sherbet has a nice, smooth consistency.

Yield: 3 to 4 servings

½ cup sugar

1¾ cups warm milk

½ cup crushed pineapple, drained

2 cups orange juice

⅛ teaspoon salt

In a large bowl, mix the sugar with the warm milk until the sugar is fully dissolved. Chill in the refrigerator for 1 hour. Add in pineapple, orange juice, and salt. Freeze until firm. Empty into a blender and pulse until smooth. Freeze 1 to 2 more hours before serving. Spoon into individual serving bowls.

Lime Sherbet
Cooler

This lime cooler, with its psychedelic shade of green, embodies the vibe of the peace-and-love movement. It's also a cinch to whip up in the blender, and it goes down smooth on a summer day. Feel free to experiment with this recipe by mixing the sherbet with other sodas, like berry-flavored seltzers or sparkling lemonade.

Yield: 1 serving

2 large scoops lime sherbet

6–8 ounces ginger ale or carbonated lemon-lime drink

1 cup ice cubes, crushed

Use a blender to combine all ingredients. The drink should be thick with ice, but not lumpy. Pour into a large glass and garnish with a slice of lemon or lime.

WOW FACTOR
Add glamour to a traditional lemon slice garnish with this simple trick: Peel a few narrow strips off a lemon going from top to bottom and discard. Slice the lemon width-wise and perch the flowery peels on the edge of a glass.

S'mores Ice Cream Sandwiches

Building these ice cream sandwiches is a breeze, but keeping them from flying off the plate is a serious challenge. This recipe transforms a simple childhood delight into a deluxe, party-friendly dessert in just a few easy steps. Choosing a double-chocolate premium ice cream for these frozen s'mores will make them even more irresistible.

Yield: 12 servings

12 graham crackers, broken into 24 squares

1 cup Marshmallow Fluff

1 quart chocolate ice cream (softened)

1½ cups Cool Whip

1 (12-ounce) jar hot fudge sauce, warmed

Place 12 squares of graham crackers on a cookie sheet lined with wax paper. Add a spoonful of marshmallow topping to each cracker. Layer on a spoonful of chocolate ice cream. Set aside.

To the remaining 12 cracker squares, add a dollop of Cool Whip to the center. Flip onto a marshmallow/ice cream cracker to make your sandwich. Repeat with remaining 11 squares. Freeze for at least 4 hours or overnight.

Place hot fudge sauce in a small, deep bowl. Remove treats from freezer and dip half of each sandwich into the hot fudge sauce. Re-freeze or enjoy as is.

CHAPTER FOUR

FROZEN PIES

Lime Rickey Freezer Pie

The lime rickey is a soda fountain classic that has been treasured for decades by nostalgic foodies and lime-lovers alike. This recipe creates a hearty frozen dessert from all the same elements of that delicious cold drink by following one of the golden rules of dessert making: Everything tastes better with crushed cookies. This recipe uses vanilla wafers for crust, but gingersnap cookies are another worthy option.

Yield: 8 to 10 servings

CRUST

1½ cups vanilla wafer cookies, crushed

2 tablespoons sugar

½ cup butter, melted

FILLING

2 pints vanilla ice cream, softened

1 pint lime sherbet, softened

1½ cups Cool Whip

8–10 fresh raspberries, for garnish

In a small bowl, combine cookies, sugar, and melted butter. Press into the bottom of a 9-inch pie dish. Freeze for 30 minutes.

In a medium bowl, mix together ice cream and sherbet. Spread onto crust and freeze for 4 hours or overnight. Frost with Cool Whip and garnish with fresh raspberries before serving.

Cookies & Cream
Sundae Pie

Let the good times roll with this fantastic frozen dish made from the best cookie on Earth. Chocolate sandwich cookies are the basis of this frozen specialty, but the ice cream flavor is yours for the choosing. Try mint chocolate chip ice cream for a fresh twist or add in strawberry for a fruity complement to the chocolate crust.

Yield: 8 to 10 servings

CRUST

1½ cups crushed chocolate sandwich cookies, about 18 cookies

2 tablespoons sugar

½ cup melted butter

FILLING

½ gallon vanilla ice cream, softened

1 tablespoon chocolate syrup

¼ cup miniature chocolate chips

In a small bowl, mix together crushed cookies, sugar, and melted butter. Press into the bottom and sides of a 9-inch pie plate. Refrigerate crust for 30 minutes.

Spread ice cream gently onto crust. Freeze for at least 4 hours, preferably overnight. Drizzle with chocolate syrup and cover in mini chocolate chips before serving.

Pink Lemonade Pie

When it comes to simple and satisfying beverages, lemonade is tops. Its fresh and inviting flavor conjures up memories of carefree summer afternoons. Combine that nostalgic, all-American flavor with a buttery graham cracker crumble and you've got the dump-and-freeze Pink Lemonade Pie. For a dose of summer refreshment, serve this treat any day, any time of year.

Yield: 12 servings

CRUST

1½ cups graham cracker crumbs

¼ cup sugar

6 tablespoons butter, melted

FILLING

1 (12-ounce) can frozen pink lemonade concentrate

1 (8-ounce) can crushed pineapple, drained

1 (14-ounce) can sweetened condensed milk

1 (8-ounce) container Cool Whip

Lemon slices, for garnish

Mix crust ingredients in a small bowl and empty into a 9 x 9-inch baking dish. Press down gently with a piece of wax paper to create an even layer. In a medium bowl, mix filling ingredients until fully blended and pour over crumbs. Freeze for approximately 4 hours or until firm. Serve with a dollop of whipped cream and a slice of lemon.

Pistachio Pudding
Ice Cream Pie

Once pistachio ice cream was introduced in the 1940s, America was hooked! Its pale green charm awarded it a place in many mid-century recipes and products, including cakes, cookies, and other sweets. This freezer-friendly recipe pays tribute to that old-fashioned flavor with the added delights of vanilla ice cream and a delicious vanilla wafer crust.

Yield: 8 to 10 servings

CRUST

1½ cups vanilla wafers, crumbled

2 tablespoons sugar

½ cup butter, melted

FILLING

2 (3.4-ounce) boxes instant pistachio pudding mix

1 cup milk

3 cups vanilla ice cream, softened

¼ cup shredded sweetened coconut, for garnish

In a small bowl, mix crumbled wafers, sugar, and melted butter. Using wax paper, press crumb mixture into bottom of a 9-inch pie dish and freeze for 30 minutes. In a large bowl, whisk together pudding mix and milk. Add ice cream and stir until well combined. Spoon ice cream mixture over crust and freeze for 4 to 5 hours. Sprinkle with shredded coconut before serving.

WOW FACTOR
You can also make a statement and add texture to this pie with a topping of toffee bits, chopped walnuts, chocolate candy bar pieces, or chocolate sprinkles.

Pumpkin Ice Cream Pie

Pumpkin pie has earned its place alongside apple pie as a great American classic. Those who remember enjoying it on special occasions as a child will love the way this dessert guides them down memory lane. With the help of a store-bought graham cracker crust, creating this dump-and-freeze dessert is as fast as it is rewarding.

Yield: 8 to 10 servings

1 quart butter pecan or vanilla ice cream, softened

¾ cup milk

1 cup canned pumpkin

½ cup light brown sugar

½ teaspoon vanilla extract

1 teaspoon pumpkin pie spice

1 (9-inch) ready-made graham cracker crust

Whipped cream, for topping

¼ cup walnuts, for topping

In a large bowl, mix together ice cream, milk, pumpkin, brown sugar, vanilla, and pumpkin pie spice. Spread mixture over crust. Freeze for 4 hours or overnight. Top with whipped cream and walnuts.

WOW FACTOR
Add some drama when you put a pie like this on display. Place it on a cake stand and let it shine. With a few artfully placed cinnamon sticks for topping, you've got a frozen treat to remember.

Boozy Mint & Fudge Pie

Be ready to slap the kids' hands away when they inevitably reach for this alcohol-infused freezer pie. Inspired by the crème de menthe drink that experienced its heyday in the mid-1950s, this frozen treat is a delicious trip back in time.

Yield: 8 to 10 servings

CRUST

1½ cups crushed chocolate sandwich cookies
or grasshopper cookies

2 tablespoons sugar

¼ cup (½ stick) unsalted butter, melted

FILLING

20 large marshmallows

⅔ cup milk

¼ cup green crème de menthe

2 tablespoons white crème de cacao

1½ cups Cool Whip

In a small bowl, mix together the cookie crumbs, sugar, and melted butter. Using wax paper, press crumb crust firmly into the bottom of a 9-inch pie pan.

Melt the marshmallows in the microwave at 15-second intervals. In a large bowl, whisk together melted marshmallows and milk until smooth. Allow to cool. Add in the crème de menthe and crème de cacao. Fold in the Cool Whip. Pour over pie crust, cover with plastic wrap, and freeze for 4 hours or more.

WOW FACTOR
This dessert screams to be sprinkled with chocolate shavings. Place a chocolate bar in the refrigerator and use a veggie peeler to create expertly curled shavings to add to the top of your frozen pie.

Coconut Cream Cloud Pie

Stay cool and collected with this refreshing, freezer-ready Coconut Cream Cloud Pie recipe. When velvety smooth coconut cream meets a crumbly, gingersnap crust, everybody wins. If time is an issue, you can use a store-bought graham cracker crust to make an even speedier version of this adorable and fluffy frozen dessert.

Yield: 8 to 10 servings

CRUST

1½ cups gingersnap cookie crumbs

⅓ cup butter, melted

2 tablespoons sugar

FILLING

1½ cups vanilla ice cream, softened

2 cups cold milk

2 (3.4-ounce) packages instant coconut cream pudding mix

1 cup Cool Whip

½ cup shredded sweetened coconut

In a medium bowl, combine the cookie crumbs, melted butter, and sugar. Press into a 9-inch pie dish and allow to set in the freezer.

In a large mixing bowl, whisk together the ice cream, milk, and pudding mix until fully combined. Let sit for 5 minutes to thicken. Spread over crust. Top with Cool Whip and coconut flakes and freeze for 4 hours or more.

Ice Cream
Lemon Pie

The retro-style beauty and simplicity of this dump-and-freeze lemon pie makes it the perfect delicacy for your next gathering. It's easy to make an impact when your primary flavor is lemon. The cool zing of this slice-and-serve specialty never fails to impress.

Yield: 8 to 10 servings

1 (10-ounce) jar lemon curd

2 tablespoons lemon juice

1 (9-inch) ready-made graham cracker crust

1½ cups pineapple chunks or tidbits, drained and divided

3 cups vanilla ice cream, softened

1½ cups Cool Whip

Slice of lemon, for garnish

In a small bowl, mix together lemon curd and lemon juice. Spread over bottom of crust and freeze until firm, approximately 45 minutes. Stir 1 cup pineapple pieces into ice cream. Spread ice cream layer over lemon curd layer. Freeze 3 to 4 hours, or until set. Top with Cool Whip and garnish with remaining pineapples and a slice of lemon, if desired.

Banana Split Ice Cream Pie

Why make a single banana split when you can make one that the whole family can enjoy together? An American favorite in pie form, this banana split dump-and-freeze dessert rewards you with rich mouthfuls of ice cream and tender layers of bananas and pineapples, plus all the toppings you loved as a kid. It will be the hit of your family dinner night.

Yield: 8 to 10 servings

CRUST

1¼ cups vanilla wafer crumbs

¾ cup walnuts, crushed

2 tablespoons sugar

⅓ cup butter, melted

FILLING

2 bananas, sliced

1 cup crushed pineapples, drained

½ gallon Neapolitan ice cream, softened

1½ cups Cool Whip

½ cup chopped walnuts

Chocolate syrup, for drizzling

Maraschino cherries for garnish

In a food processor, blend wafer crumbs, walnuts, and sugar. Drizzle in melted butter and mix by hand. Press into a 9-inch pie dish using wax paper to form an even layer. Freeze for 30 minutes.

Arrange a layer of sliced bananas over chilled crust. Spread crushed pineapple over bananas. Add softened ice cream and press gently into an even layer. Top with Cool Whip. Freeze until firm. Sprinkle with walnuts. Drizzle with chocolate syrup if desired and garnish with maraschino cherries before serving.

CHAPTER FIVE

FROZEN CAKES

Pineapple Upside-Down Freezer Cake

Summer gatherings turn delightfully tropical with the addition of this easy-to-make pineapple cake. Use ladyfingers as a starting point and build upward with layers of creamy pineapple and spongy cookies until you have a dessert that's ready to freeze and serve.

Yield: 8 to 10 servings

2 (3-ounce) packages ladyfingers or margherite cookies, broken into halves

1 (3.4-ounce) box instant vanilla pudding mix

1 (8-ounce) container Cool Whip, divided

1 (20-ounce) can pineapple tidbits, drained

½ cup maraschino cherries, halved

Line a loaf pan with plastic wrap. Arrange ladyfingers along sides and bottom of pan. In a large bowl, mix together pudding mix and 2½ cups Cool Whip. Stir in most of the pineapples and cherries (setting aside a few pieces of fruit for garnish). Spoon half of the fruit mixture into the loaf pan, filling it about halfway. Add a layer of ladyfingers and top with remaining pineapple mixture. Cover and freeze for 4 to 6 hours before serving. To serve, invert over a serving platter and garnish with remaining Cool Whip and fruit.

WOW FACTOR

When presenting a frozen cake, consider using canned whipped cream to create a fluffy white border around the cake itself. Add a maraschino cherry to the border every few inches for a pop of color.

Berry Blast
Sponge Cake

This frozen masterpiece features one of the guiltiest pleasures of all time: the Twinkie. Freeze some in advance for easy slicing and they become the foundation of your next dump-and-freeze cake. Layer on some fresh berries and a thick layer of vanilla ice cream and you've got yourself a treat that's fit for a regular day or a big celebration.

Yield: 12 servings

10 Twinkies, frozen

2 cups fresh or frozen berries

1 gallon vanilla ice cream, softened

1 (8-ounce) container Cool Whip

Slice Twinkies in half lengthwise (this is easier if they're frozen) and lay evenly, flat side up, in a 9 x 13-inch baking pan. Scatter 1 cup of berries over the top of the Twinkies. In a large bowl, combine ice cream and Cool Whip. Spread over berries. Add remaining berries to the top of the ice cream layer. Freeze until firm.

Rainbow Sherbet Layer Cake

This brilliant treat lets you hide colorful layers of sherbet in a ready-made angel food cake. Custom-color whipped frosting makes for an irresistible touch of fun. This treat makes a perfect last-minute birthday cake, but you'll find yourself coming up with excuses to make it more often! For easier preparation, freeze the angel food cake before preparing this dessert so you can slice it without any trouble.

Yield: 9 servings

CAKE

1 prepared angel food cake

3 cups rainbow sherbet, softened

FROSTING

1 (8-ounce) container Cool Whip

Food coloring of your choice, optional

Rainbow sprinkles

Cut angel food cake into slices approximately ½-inch thick. Arrange slices to cover the bottom of a 9 x 9-inch square baking dish. Scoop sherbet onto cake slices and press gently with wax paper to create an even layer. Top with remaining cake slices. Add food coloring, if desired, to Cool Whip tub and mix well. Frost cake with a thick layer of whipped topping. Add rainbow sprinkles. Freeze for 1 hour or until firm. Remove from freezer 15 to 20 minutes before serving.

Banana Wafer Cake

This is the kind of recipe that was printed on the back of a pudding box in the 1950s. Every time you opened the pantry, it would be calling to you. Get ready to revive the winning taste combination of creamy bananas and fluffy vanilla wafers and share it with your family. You can use a regular store-bought pie crust for this recipe, but this tasty pecan-wafer crust is worth the extra few minutes it takes to create.

Yield: 8 to 10 servings

CRUST

1¼ cups vanilla wafer cookies, crushed and divided

¾ cup pecans, crushed

2 tablespoons melted butter

FILLING

3 large bananas, sliced

1 box of instant vanilla or banana pudding mix

1 cup cold milk

¾ cup Cool Whip

Chocolate syrup, for drizzling

In a small bowl, mix together 1 cup crushed vanilla wafers, pecans, and melted butter. Press crumb mixture into the bottom of a 9-inch glass pie dish.

Arrange half of the banana slices to cover the bottom of the pie crust. Whisk together pudding mix and milk until pudding thickens. Pour over banana layer. Add remaining banana slices to the top of the pudding. Sprinkle with remaining ¼ cup of vanilla wafers. Freeze for 3 to 4 hours. Add Cool Whip and a drizzle of chocolate syrup before serving.

Cookies & Cream Cake

This recipe never disappoints. If you want to finish off a meal with flavors that bring out the kid in everyone, crumble and whip your way to this chocolaty frozen delight. Add a topping of fresh, sliced strawberries or a sprinkle of chocolate chips to make this recipe your own.

Yield: 12 servings

CRUST

2¼ cups chocolate sandwich cookies (about 24), crushed, divided

½ cup (1 stick) butter, melted

FILLING

1 (8-ounce) package cream cheese, softened

1 cup powdered sugar

1 (12-ounce) container Cool Whip, divided

1 (5.1-ounce) package chocolate fudge instant pudding mix

3 cups cold milk

Mix together 2 cups crushed cookies and melted butter. Press mixture into the bottom of a greased 9 x 13-inch baking pan.

In a large bowl, with an electric mixer at medium speed, beat together the cream cheese and powdered sugar. Add in half of the Cool Whip. Spread over crust and refrigerate for 30 minutes. Whisk together pudding mix and milk until pudding forms. Pour over chilled cream cheese layer. Refrigerate for 1 hour. Frost with remaining 6 ounces of Cool Whip and sprinkle with ¼ cup reserved cookie crumbs.

Index

BONUS!

DOLLAR SAVING DINNER RECIPES FROM

AVAILABLE EVERYWHERE BOOKS ARE SOLD!

Chicken and Broccoli Casserole

This is a simple, speedy recipe to prepare when you're rushing to make dinner and resisting the temptation to order take-out. With just five ingredients, it's easy to make this casserole and still stay within your weekly budget. For extra savings, divide this casserole into two smaller dishes so you can serve one and freeze the other for later.

Yield: 8 servings

3–4 boneless skinless chicken breasts or thighs, cubed and cooked

1 bunch fresh broccoli (or 4 cups broccoli), steamed

2 (16-ounce) jars Alfredo sauce, warmed

4 cups shredded mozzarella and/or cheddar cheese

1 (16-ounce) box penne pasta, cooked

Preheat oven to 350°F. Add cooked chicken, broccoli, Alfredo sauce, and 2 cups cheese to saucepan and stir. Stir in cooked pasta. Spray or grease a 9 x 13-inch casserole dish. Empty saucepan mixture into baking dish. Sprinkle 2 cups cheese on top. Bake for about 10 minutes or until cheese melts.

Slow Cooker Pot Roast

A crafty cook knows how to take a few shortcuts in the interest of time and money without sacrificing on flavor. This simple slow cooker pot roast recipe will satisfy a large family and then some! Freeze the leftovers so you can enjoy it again any time you want.

Yield: 10 servings

½ cup steak sauce

½ cup water

1 (9-ounce) package onion-mushroom soup mix

1 (approximately 2½-pound) boneless beef chuck eye roast

1 pound potatoes

1 (16-ounce) bag baby carrots

1 (16-ounce) bag green beans

1 onion, thickly sliced

Mix first 3 ingredients until blended. Place meat in slow cooker; top with vegetables and sauce. Cover with lid. Cook on low for 8 to 9 hours (or on high for 6 to 7 hours).

Find affordable substitutes for expensive recipe ingredients. For example, cranberry juice and chicken stock can both be used in place of red wine.